D1369209

POCKET
PRAYERS
OF BLESSING

Other books in the series:

Pocket Celtic Prayers
Compiled by Martin Wallace

Pocket Graces
Compiled by Pam Robertson

Pocket Prayers for Children
Compiled by Christopher Herbert

Pocket Prayers: The Classic Edition
Compiled by Christopher Herbert

Pocket Prayers for Advent and Christmas
Compiled by Jan McFarlane

Pocket Prayers for Commuters
Compiled by Christopher Herbert

Pocket Prayers for Healing and Wholeness
Compiled by Trevor Lloyd

Pocket Prayers for Marriage
Compiled by Andrew and Pippa Body

Pocket Prayers for Parents
Compiled by Hamish and Sue Bruce

Pocket Words of Comfort
Compiled by Christopher Herbert

Pocket Prayers for Pilgrims
Compiled by John Pritchard

POCKET
PRAYERS
OF BLESSING

COMPILED BY
JAN McFARLANE

CHURCH HOUSE
PUBLISHING

Church House Publishing
Church House
Great Smith Street
London SW1P 3AZ

ISBN 978 0 7151 4239 4

Published 2012 by Church House Publishing

Email: copyright@churchofengland.org.uk

Designed by www.penguinboy.net

Printed in England by Ashford Colour Press Ltd, Fareham, Hants

CONTENTS

INTRODUCTION

It has long been a tradition among Christians to 'count your blessings' before sleep. In our prayers before our heads hit the pillow, we thank God for the day that is passed; say sorry for the things we've done wrong, or failed to do; pray for those we've encountered, and bring to mind the many ways in which God has blessed us. Because God longs to bless us. In Matthew's Gospel, Jesus reminds us that we, who get it wrong so often, know how to give our children good things, and wouldn't dream of giving them a stone if they ask for bread. 'How much more, then, will your Father in heaven give good things to those who ask him!'

If we count our blessings, and open our eyes to all the good things God has given us and done for us, noticing especially the smallest things we so often take for granted, we soon find ourselves blessing, or praising, or thanking God in return. And then, grateful for all we have received, we set out to bring God's blessing to others. Or at least, that's the plan!

This little book is a collection of prayers asking God's blessing on the people we meet day by day, as well as on the more unusual situations we encounter from time to time. In asking God to bless, we're asking for his protection and his help. We're asking God to be present and to make a difference, even if we can't always immediately spot God's hand at work.

In the Roman Catholic, Orthodox and Anglican Church, priests are given the authority to bless. There are special occasions when a priest's blessing will be called for, such as at a wedding, or at the time of death. But in the Bible, blessing is part of everyday life and it seems as if anyone could ask God's blessing on another. This book follows the convention of preserving the 'you' form of blessing for priests, and using the 'us' form of blessing for every one of us to use. The priest says 'God bless you' but all of us can say 'May God bless us'. In addition, 'he' and 'she' are used interchangeably, and N gives the opportunity to insert the name of the one for whom we are praying.

My prayer is that this little book, which will slip so easily into your jacket pocket, cassock pocket, bag or briefcase, will be of help to you as you share God's blessing at all times and in all places and with all you meet. For the more we see God's blessing at work, the more skilled we will become in the art of blessing God in return.

'I will bless you
so that you will be a blessing.'
Genesis 12:2

AT ALL TIMES AND IN ALL PLACES

God's blessing surrounds us wherever we are and whatever our circumstances and God is near to us even when we can't feel his presence. The teachings of Jesus which we call the Beatitudes remind us that it is sometimes in the most unlikely places and situations that we experience God's blessing. The prayers and reflections in this chapter can be used at any time and in any place to remind us of God's presence.

Bless the Lord, O my soul,
and all that is within me bless his holy name.

Psalm 103

Prayer fastens the soul to God, making it one with his will through the deep inward working of the Holy Spirit. So he says this, 'Pray inwardly, even though you feel no joy in it. For it does good, though you feel nothing, see nothing, yes, even though you think you cannot pray. For when you are dry and empty, sick and weak, your prayers please me, though there be little enough to please you. All believing prayer is precious in my sight.' God accepts the good-will and work of his servants, no matter how we feel.

Julian of Norwich (1342–1413)

God gets down on his knees among us, gets on our level and shares himself with us. He does not reside afar off and send us diplomatic messages; he kneels among us. That posture is characteristic of God ... God shares himself generously and graciously.

Eugene Peterson

Deep peace of the Running Wave to you.
Deep peace of the Flowing Air to you.
Deep peace of the Quiet Earth to you.
Deep peace of the Shining Stars to you.
Deep peace of the Son of Peace to you.

Celtic Benediction

Lord Jesus,
take my mind and think through me,
take my hands and bless through me,
take my mouth and speak through me;
above all, Lord Jesus,
take my spirit and pray in me;
so that it is you who move and have your being in me.

Book of Hours (Sixteenth Century)

May the peace of God
which passes all understanding,
keep our hearts and minds
in the knowledge and love of Jesus Christ our Lord;
and may the blessing of God Almighty,
the Father, the Son and the Holy Spirit
be upon us and remain with us always.

Based on Philippians 4:7

May God bless us with discomfort at easy answers,
half truths, superficial relationships,
so that we may live deep within our hearts.

May God bless us with anger at injustice,
oppression and exploitation of people,
so that we may work for justice, equality and peace.

May God bless us with tears to shed
for those who suffer from pain, rejection, starvation
and war
so that we may reach out our hands to comfort them
and turn their pain to joy.

And may God bless us with the foolishness
to think that we can make a difference in the world,
so that we will do the things
which others tell us cannot be done.

Source unknown

The guarding of the God of life be on us,
the guarding of the loving Christ be on us,
the guarding of the Holy Spirit be on us,
every day and night,
to aid us and enfold us,
each day, each night. Amen
Church of Scotland

May the blessing of God,
the eternal goodwill of God,
the shalom of God,
the wildness and the warmth of God,
be among us and between us,
now and always.
St Hilda Community

May the Lord bless us and watch over us;
the Lord make his face shine upon us
and be gracious to us;
the Lord look kindly on us and give us peace. Amen.
Common Worship

The Beatitudes

Blessed are the poor in spirit,
for theirs is the kingdom of heaven.

Blessed are those who mourn,
for they will be comforted.

Blessed are the meek,
for they will inherit the earth.

Blessed are those who hunger and thirst for
righteousness,
for they will be filled.

Blessed are the merciful,
for they will receive mercy.

Blessed are the pure in heart,
for they will see God.

Blessed are the peacemakers,
for they will be called children of God.

Blessed are those who are persecuted for
righteousness' sake,
for theirs is the kingdom of heaven.

Blessed are you when people revile you
and persecute you
and utter all kinds of evil against you
falsely on my account.
Rejoice and be glad,
for your reward is great in heaven,
for in the same way they persecuted
the prophets who were before you.

Matthew 5:3–11 from The New Revised Standard Version

The Beatitudes (A modern interpretation)

You're blessed when you're at the end of your rope.
With less of you there is more of God and his rule.

You're blessed when you feel
you've lost what is most dear to you.
Only then can you be embraced
by the One most dear to you.

You're blessed when you're content
with just who you are
no more, no less.
That's the moment you find yourselves
proud owners of everything that can't be bought.

You're blessed when you've worked up
a good appetite for God.
He's food and drink in the best meal you'll ever eat.

You're blessed when you care.
At the moment of being 'care-full,'
you find yourselves cared for.

You're blessed when you get your inside world
your mind and heart – put right.
Then you can see God in the outside world.

You're blessed when you can show
people how to cooperate instead of compete or fight.
That's when you discover who you really are,
and your place in God's family.

You're blessed when your commitment to God
provokes persecution.
The persecution drives you even deeper
into God's kingdom.

Not only that – count yourselves blessed every time
people put you down or throw you out or speak lies
about you to discredit me. What it means is that the
truth is too close for comfort and they are
uncomfortable. You can be glad when that happens –
give a cheer, even! – for though they don't like it, I do!
And all heaven applauds. And know that you are in
good company. My prophets and witnesses have
always gotten into this kind of trouble.

Matthew 5:3–11 from The Message

THE DAILY ROUND

It is said that on the morning of the first battle of the first English Civil War, Jacob Astley, who was to lead the combat, prayed 'Lord I shall be very busy this day. If I forget thee, do not thou forget me.' Beginning and ending our day by remembering God's presence with us means that even if our days are inexpressibly busy, we can be confident of God's blessing on all that we do and say. Some of the prayers in this chapter are short enough to be learned by heart – a blessing in themselves for households where there isn't a quiet moment in the rush to get to work and to school.

ON RISING

My Father, for another night
of quiet sleep and rest,
for all the joy of morning light,
thy holy name be blest.

H W Baker (1821–1877)

Be thou a bright flame before me,
Be thou a guiding star above me,
Be thou a smooth path below me,
Be thou a kindly shepherd behind me,
Today, tonight, and for ever.

St Columba (c521–597)

I am blessed, I am blessed.
Every day of my life I am blessed.
When I wake up in the morning,
when I lay my head to rest,
I am blessed, I am blessed.

Traditional

Christ has
no body now on earth but yours,
no hands but yours,
no feet but yours.
Yours are the eyes
through which Christ's compassion
cares for the people of the world;
yours are the feet
with which Christ is to go about doing good;
yours are the hands
through which Christ now brings a blessing.

So I promise this day
to keep awake,
to live each moment to the full,
to look with eyes of compassion,
and to act with kindness.

Teresa of Avila and Jim Cotter

BEFORE A MEAL

Bless, O Lord, this food to our use
and ourselves to your service,
and make us mindful of the needs of others.

Traditional

Praise God from whom all blessings flow,
praise him all creatures here below,
praise him above, ye heavenly host.
praise Father, Son and Holy Ghost.

Thomas Ken (1637–1711)

Come, Lord Jesus, be our guest.
Let this food to us be blest.

Traditional

All good gifts around us
are sent from heaven above;
then thank the Lord, O thank the Lord
for all his love. Amen.

Matthias Claudius (1740–1815)

Father, for this food we're about to receive,
and for all those who've been involved
in every stage of its preparation,
we give you thanks, in Jesus' name. Amen.

For every cup and plateful,
God make us truly grateful.
Anon

God bless these our tables, our food and our wine;
remember at Cana they had a good time;
and may our compassion be well nourished today
as we care for the anxious we meet on life's way.
Amen.
Bishop Graham James

BEFORE SLEEP

Before the ending of the day,
creator of the world, we pray
that you, with steadfast love, would keep
your watch around us while we sleep.

From evil dreams defend our sight,
from fears and terrors of the night;
tread underfoot our deadly foe
that we no sinful thought may know.

O Father, that we ask be done
through Jesus Christ, your only Son;
and Holy Spirit, by whose breath
our souls are raised to life from death.

Common Worship: Night Prayer

Blessing, light and glory surround us
and scatter the darkness
of the long and lonely night.

Jim Cotter

Bless to us, O God,
the moon that is above us,
the earth that is beneath us,
the friends who are around us,
your image deep within us.
the rest which is before us. Amen.

Iona Community

I will both lie down and sleep in peace;
for you alone, O Lord, make me lie down in safety.

Psalm 4:8 NRSV

THE COMMON TASK

It's easy to think of prayer as something which belongs to time in church, or possibly for the beginning and the end of the day, and just possibly before meals. But we don't always think to pray in the midst of a busy working day. God is as present in the hustle and bustle of the office, shop and factory floor as he is in the peace of an ancient church or the quietness of the garden in the early morning. The prayers in this chapter can help us to remember God's blessing in the 'earthquake, wind and fire' as well as in the still small voice of calm.

Let the favour of the Lord our God be upon us,
and prosper for us the work of our hands.
Psalm 90:17 NRSV

AT THE BEGINNING
OF A WORKING DAY

Lord, you know the pressures of this day,
the appointments, the phone calls,
the constant ping of emails,
the insistent demands on my time and energy.
Bless me with calmness and courtesy,
patience and peacefulness,
and may I see in all I meet this day
the image of your glory. Amen

AT THE CLOSE OF A WORKING DAY

I've done my best, Lord.
Forgive what I've failed to do.
Bless my efforts and the people I've met
Especially ...
I leave it all in your hands, to your care and protection.
May I return home with a sense of peace
knowing that you'll give me rest and refreshment
and strength to face the demands of another day.

BEFORE A PHONE CALL

Father God, please bless this call.
May the caller feel heard, understood, encouraged.
Amen.

BEFORE A MEETING

God of peace, we ask your blessing on our meeting.
Help us to set aside our busyness
and focus on the task at hand.
Give us wisdom, discernment and integrity,
boldness to speak and a willingness to listen.
Keep us mindful of those our decisions will affect,
and may all our deliberations be to your glory.

BEFORE A MORE DIFFICULT MEETING

Be present with us now, O God,
and help us to focus on the task at hand.
Keep our defences low,
our integrity high,
our compassion broad,
our procrastination narrow.
Please bless the gift of this time together,
for our good, and the good of those we serve.

AT THE END
OF A MEETING

O God, when two or three
are gathered together in your name,
you promise to be there with them.
Bless all we have discussed,
the people our decisions will affect,
and us as we travel home.
May the work we have done in your name
be for your sake and for your glory. Amen.

FOR A NEW COLLEAGUE

God of new beginnings, bless *N*
as she joins our *team / office / workplace*.
May she find a warm welcome.
As we remember the nervous anticipation,
the confusion and the exhaustion of a new beginning,
help us to remember that her arrival
means change for us too.
Protect us from defensiveness
and make us warm and generous colleagues,
as we reflect your welcome for the stranger
who may well become a friend. Amen.

FOR A NEW COMPUTER

Creator God, thank you for the skill
and the vision of those who created this computer.
Thank you for the world it will open up to me.
Help those who use such technology
for destructive desires, for escapism, for harm,
to find help and healing.
Please bless this computer and may it be used
for creative work, for the nurturing of relationships,
for constructive pleasure,
for the building of a better world.
For I ask in Jesus' name. Amen.

ON HEARING OF A REDUNDANCY

God of mercy, bless N as he comes to terms
with the loss of his job.
Be close to him as he faces an uncertain future.
Be with his family and friends as they support him
through this sudden bereavement.
And in the fullness of time, open to him
new doors, new opportunities, new beginnings. Amen.

MARKING THE MILESTONES

God's blessing can be invoked for the milestones – the moments in life's journey of special significance. Such moments often involve chance, and change can be both uncomfortable and unsettling. If we remember God's presence in every aspect of our lives, he promises to guard us with his peace.

And remember, I am with you always,
even to the end of the age.
Matthew 28:20 RSV

FOR A
NEW-BORN BABY

Bless the one who carried you
and pushed you into our world.
Grant her healing, peace
and strength of mind and body.

Bless those who receive you
as a new member of their family.
Fill them with thanksgiving
and equip them with special skills
for the privilege and responsibility of caring for you.

May the Creator God protect you.
May the love of Christ encompass you.
May the power of the Spirit enliven you
Today and always.
Heather Johnston

FOR A BIRTHDAY

Lord God, please bless *N* as he celebrates his birthday.
Be with him as he recalls the day of his birth
and gives thanks for those who gave him life.
May this day be one of joy and celebration,
and, as he looks ahead to another year,
be with him on the journey. Amen.

FOR A NEW PET

God of creation, you give us animals
to be our helpers, companions, friends.
Please bless our family as *N* joins us.
Thank you for the joy and life she will bring.
May we care for her, enjoy her, respect her,
in reflection of your care for us.

FOR A CHILD STARTING SCHOOL

Loving Father, please bless *N*
as he sets out to school for the first time,
and takes his next step
in the life-long adventure of learning.

Bless the teachers and schools staff
as they welcome him and nurture him.
Give them patience, understanding and wisdom.

Bless the children he will meet;
those he'll find difficult to encounter
and those who will be friends for life.

And bless his parents as they let him go,
as they too begin the next chapter
of their family life. Amen.

FOR A NEW SCHOOL TERM

Dear God, thank you for the holidays
and for times of rest and relaxation.
Be with me now as I prepare
to go back to school for another term.
I feel a bit nervous, I don't know why!
But you understand.
Help me to sleep well, and wake refreshed
Ready to grasp with both hands
all the opportunities that will come my way. Amen.

FOR A STUDENT

God the Creator, permeate my mind;
God the Son, enlighten my search for truth;
God the Spirit kindle my desire for discovery;
God the Holy Trinity bless my curiosity and
my concentration
this day and always.

Michael Turnbull

ON GOING TO COLLEGE OR UNIVERSITY

Father God, bless N
as this new chapter opens
in the story of her life.
Please bless her with the gift of new friends.
Please bless her with opportunities for learning.
Please bless her with enriching activity.
And above all, keep her safe
under the shadow of your wing. Amen.

BEFORE AN EXAM

Wise God, please bless N as she sits her exam.
Help her to remember all she has learned.
Protect her from worry, stress and panic;
give her a calm mind, confidence and energy;
just enough adrenalin – but not too much.
May she give of her very best
then rest
knowing it's in your hands. Amen.

BEFORE COLLECTING EXAM RESULTS

Dear God, I feel sick.
Please bless N as she collects her results.
And whatever the outcome may be
may I model your patience, your understanding,
your unconditional love. Amen.

BEFORE AN INTERVIEW

Loving God, please bless N
as she goes for her interview.
Help her to remain calm and poised,
clear minded and confident.
Please bless those she will encounter today,
and whatever the outcome,
help her to know your guiding presence
as your will for her unfolds. Amen.

ON HEARING OF AN ENGAGEMENT

God of love, please bless *N* and *N*
as they prepare for the commitment of marriage.
May the plans for the wedding not overtake
the more important preparation
for their lifetime together.
Please bless their family and friends
as they prepare for this special day
and may your blessing be upon them now and always.
Amen.

FOR A WEDDING ANNIVERSARY

God of celebration, please bless N and N
as they commemorate this special day.
Thank you for being alongside them
for better for worse; for richer, for poorer
in sickness and in health.
Help them to set aside the petty irritations
and the trivial skirmishes of daily life,
so that they may celebrate the mystery of love
and cherish each other until their life's end. Amen.

ON HEARING THE NEWS OF A PREGNANCY

Father God, as we celebrate this happy news,
please surround with your blessing *N*
and her unborn child.
Protect them both
and bring them safely through to the moment of birth.
Please bless *N* (father) as he cares for them both
and prepares for the extra responsibilities
parenthood brings.
As their child grows in the warmth of the womb
may the warmth of their love for each other
expand to embrace their little one.

FOR THE ADOPTION OF A CHILD

Father God, you have made us
your sons and daughters through adoption.
Please bless N and N as they prepare
to welcome N into their home.
May their adopted son/daughter know, through them,
safety and security, acceptance and love.
Please bless N and N with wisdom and patience
for all the joys and the challenges of family life,
as they nurture N into adulthood and beyond.

ON FACING RETIREMENT

God of the past, the present and the future,
the retirement I once longed for looks scarier now.
Be with me as I work through my fears
of not being needed;
as I let go of the role which has defined me;
as I carve out a new identity,
and renegotiate neglected relationships.
Please bless me, loving Father,
and help me to find my future in you.

ON MOVING INTO A NURSING HOME

Eternal God, you have promised never to leave us,
never to forsake us.
Please bless *N* as he prepares for the upheaval
of his move.
Bless his (children/friends) as they help,
and as they cope with their own mixed emotions
on this most difficult of days.
Bless those who will care for *N*
and may he soon know peace and comfort
as he adjusts and settles in.
Please bless him with new friendships,
and may his new surroundings soon feel like home.

ON HEARING OF A DEATH

O God, your Son suffered death
then rose from the grave,
so that we too may rise with him;
thank you that for N, suffering and pain
are no more.
May he rest in peace and rise in glory.
Bless his family and friends in their sorrow and pain.
May they be sustained by their love for each other,
as they face the difficult days that lie ahead.

Give rest, O Christ, to your servants, with your saints,
where sorrow and pain are no more, neither sighing
but life everlasting.
Russian Orthodox Kontakion of the Departed

BEFORE A FUNERAL

Jesus, you wept for your brother Lazarus.
Be close to all who mourn the death of *N*
as we gather for his funeral.
Bless the minister who will guide us,
and help us to hear your words of comfort, hope
and peace.
Help *N*'s family to know the support of friends
and give them strength to face the days that lie ahead.

JOURNEYING ON

When we pause to think about it, travelling is a risky occupation. But if we didn't take the risk, we would miss out on so many opportunities, and would never truly appreciate the wonders of our lonely yet infinitely beautiful planet. It has long been the tradition to offer the journey to God and to seek his blessing.

If I take the wings of the morning
and settle at the farthest limits of the sea,
even there your hand shall lead me,
and your right hand shall hold me fast.

Psalm 139:9–10 NRSV

BEFORE A JOURNEY

May God, who is present in sunrise and nightfall,
and in the crossing of the sea,
guide our feet as we go.

May God who is with us when we sit
and when we stand,
encompass us with love
and lead us by the hand.

May God who knows our paths,
and the places where we rest,
be with us in our waiting,
be our good news for sharing
and lead us in the way that is everlasting. Amen.

The Iona Community

May the road rise to meet you.
May the wind be always at your back.
May the sun shine warm upon your face,
the rains fall soft upon your fields
and, until we meet again,
may God hold you in the palm of his hand.

An Irish Blessing

FOR A NEW CAR

Lord God, in our excitement
over the purchase of this car,
keep us ever mindful of its power.
Please bless those who drive it,
all who will be passengers.
Keep us steady and safe,
courteous and responsible.
For we ask in Jesus' name. Amen.

FOR THE PERSON OPPOSITE ON A TRAIN

To me you are anonymous
   God calls you by name

To me you are a mystery
   God knows your every breath

To me your destiny is unknown
   God guide you safely there

And may his blessing be yours, now and always.
Michael Turnbull

BEFORE A FLIGHT

God of the heavens, creator of clouds,
who gives warmth to the sun, light to the stars;
please bless us and all who journey with us.
Give grace to the stewards, wisdom to the pilot,
and grant us swift flight, safe passage, calm landing.

BEFORE A JOURNEY BY BOAT

Jesus, Lord of wind and waves,
the sea is so big, our boat is so small.
Please bless us with safe passage. Amen.

FOR A RETREAT OR QUIET DAY

God of the Sabbath, please bless me
as I take time out to spend with you.
Please bless those I have left behind;
the tasks I have left undone.
Help me to slow down, to use this time wisely,
to drink in the peace, to listen to your voice.
Nurture me, re-create me,
energize me, give me fresh vision,
so I may leave this place
ready to give you my all. Amen.

AT THE END OF A RETREAT OR QUIET DAY

God, thank you for this place
and for being present with me here.
Thank you for renewing me,
for giving me fresh vision,
for equipping me for the next stage
of the journey.
Please bless all who *live/work/minister* here,
and bless me as I go back into the world.
May my life be a witness to your presence;
may my words bring your peace and healing;
may all I encounter see a child of God,
loved unconditionally, blessed for all eternity. Amen.

IN TIMES OF TROUBLE

People who have perhaps never really prayed before often do so when faced with a difficult situation or with the prospect of illness or death. God is always ready to listen even if he may not have heard our voice much before. But what to pray? We may find old traditional prayers useful. Usually though, honesty is the best policy. If God really is, as the Bible says, our parent, then we can tell him everything. And if we're angry with the situation we can tell him so. We don't have to be on our best behavior when we approach God in times of need.

For I am convinced that neither death, nor life,
nor angels, not rulers,
nor things present, nor things to come,
nor powers, nor height. not depth,
nor anything else in all creation,
will be able to separate us from the love of God.

Romans 8:38 NRSV

WHEN DEALING WITH A DIFFICULT SITUATION

God of wisdom and of grace
please bless me as we deal with *(name situation)*.
Help me to know what to do.
Help me not to panic; nor to react without thinking.
Please send your Holy Spirit on me
and give me right judgment,
calm thinking, deep wisdom.
Help me to trust in you,
my protector and my strength.

WHEN WEARY

Lord, I'm tired;
but there's still so much to do.
Help me to focus on each and every task
as if it were my last.
Help me to understand
that you only ask of me
what you know I can handle.
And so please bless me
as I stagger on, rejoicing
in your company. Amen.

FOLLOWING A MISCARRIAGE

Compassionate God, please bless *N* and *N*
as they face their loss;
as they cope with broken hopes and dreams;
as they look towards an unknown future.
Surround them with compassionate friends
willing to listen, unembarrassed by tears.
Help them to grieve for all they have lost.
May they find comfort and strength in you. Amen.

FOR A TROUBLED RELATIONSHIP

Jesus said, 'Blessed are the peacemakers
for they shall be called the children of God.'
Please bless us, God of peace, as we try to
bring understanding and compassion
to this painful and difficult situation.
Help us not to react defensively
but to be slow to speak and quick to listen.
Please bring healing and resolution,
for we ask in the name of the prince of peace,
our Saviour, Jesus Christ. Amen.

ON HEARING OF A SEPARATION OR DIVORCE

God of love and compassion
surround with your blessing N and N
as they mourn the death of their relationship.
Keep them free from bitterness,
from destructive speech, from angry exchanges;
and in the fullness of time
may they both know healing and resurrection. Amen.

FOR ONE SUFFERING FROM DEPRESSION

God of healing, please bless *N*
in the depths of her despair.
I don't know what to say.
My words sound empty and glib.
Help me to stay close to *N*
even when she doesn't respond.
Help her to know that I care
by my silent companionship.
Help me to be to her a visible sign
of your invisible presence,
until she emerges once more from the shadows
into the glorious light of day.

WAITING FOR HOSPITAL TEST RESULTS

God of compassion and care,
please bless N as he waits for his results.
You know him inside out –
his fear and his anxiety,
in that dreadful no-man's land of not-knowing.
Please bless the medical staff as they care for him.
And, whatever the outcome,
give him a very real sense of your presence,
your courage, your strength and your peace.

ON HEARING
OF A SUICIDE

Loving God, please bless N's family
as they come to terms with the news of his death.
It's so hard to imagine his state of mind;
his desperate need to bring an end to his life.
His family will be numbed, shocked, angered.
Their questions will last them a lifetime.
But may N now know the peace of your presence.
And in time, may his family find peace of mind.
Bless them and hold them close to you,
God of the bewildered, the confused, the bereft.

FOR A VICTIM OF CRIME

Father God, your Son knew how it felt
to suffer at the hands of those who wished him evil.
Surround N with your protection and blessing.
Give him such a sense of your presence
through the love and support of family and friends,
that he will be helped to rise
above his anger and distress
and find peace and the promise of a new beginning.

ON HEARING AN AMBULANCE

God of mercy, please bless those paramedics
as they speed to the aid of someone in need.
Give them safe passage, calm minds, swift response,
and bring healing and peace to those they tend. Amen.

ON HEARING A POLICE SIREN

God of calm and order, of justice and of mercy,
please bless those police officers
as they speed to someone's aid.
Give them a right authority,
wisdom and integrity,
and bring them safely home. Amen.

ON THE DEATH OF A PET

Father God, not many will understand
the depth of our distress at the loss
of our beloved pet, *N*.
But we know that you understand.
Thank you for all that *N* meant to us,
for his companionship, warmth, affection and joy.
Please bless us and comfort us as we mourn.
We know that you, who see even the fall of a sparrow,
won't underestimate our loss. Amen.

FOR THE BURIAL OF A PET

Creator God, you make all things
and rejoice in their creation.
Thank you for the many blessings
we have received through the *N*'s life;
for the fun and happiness he brought;
for his companionship
and the comfort of his presence.
We now return his body to the earth
from which it was made.
In our sorrow, give us the blessing
of your peace
and the consolation of
so many happy memories. Amen.

FOR A HOME

Moving house is one of the most stressful and difficult of experiences, even if we're looking forward to the move. We suddenly realize just how much we depend on the stability of familiar surroundings to help us to manage all that life can throw at us.

Your parish priest may be asked to visit your new home to bless it. S/he may find these prayers useful and can adapt them accordingly. Alternatively you may wish to pray these prayers around your home.

Lord you have been our dwelling place
in all generations ...
From everlasting to everlasting, you are God.
Psalm 90:1 NRSV

FOR A NEW HOUSE

The Entrance
Welcoming God, your Son found rest
at the home of Mary and Martha,
and their brother, Lazarus.
Please bless all who enter this *(porch/hall/doorway)*;
may they know warmth and companionship;
and keep far from this door any who would wish us
harm.
For we ask in Jesus' name. Amen.

The Kitchen

Nurturing God, you feed your children with
bread from heaven, fruit of the vine, water of life.
We ask your blessing on the heart of our home.
May it ever be a source of nourishment
for body, mind and soul.
In serving, may we allow ourselves to be served,
and in giving, may we receive
from the abundance of your grace. Amen.

The Dining Room

Generous God, your Son had supper with his friends
on the night he was betrayed;
and met them for breakfast
when he rose from the grave.
We ask your blessing on this room of sharing,
of celebrations and of special occasions.
For better, for worse, in darkness and in daytime,
keep us hospitable, companionable, friends. Amen.

The Lounge / Sitting Room

God of re-creation,
please bless all who will rest in this room.
May it be a place of gathering and of sharing,
of laughter and of story-telling
May none who enter here go sad away. Amen.

The Study

God, the Word of life, please bless
all words read, written and spoken in this study.
May it be a place of learning and creativity.
May all who work here, leave better equipped
for the building of your kingdom
in this place where you have set us. Amen.

The Bathroom

Cleansing God, you wash us in the waters of baptism
and make us whiter than snow.
Bless all who will enjoy here
invigorating showers and relaxing baths.,
May we never take for granted
that most precious gift of water,
without which nothing can live. Amen.

The Bedroom

The psalmist said, 'I will lie down and take my rest;
for you, O Lord, make me dwell in safety.'
God of the still, small voice, who created the night
to be a time of restful and restorative sleep,
please bless those who will find in this room
security and a refuge from the clamour of the day.
May they sleep safely and deeply
and rise refreshed with the dawning of the day. Amen.

A Child's Bedroom

Father God, may this bedroom be to N
a place of refuge and of rest.
May your blessing be on this room,
driving far from it any fear of the dark,
for the darkness is as light to you,
and the night is as clear as the day. Amen.

A Guest Room

Hospitable God, please bless this room
that all who rest here may find
comfort, warmth and peace,
and, in time, go on their way
renewed, restored, refreshed. Amen.

Final Prayer

Visit, Lord, we pray, this place
and drive far from it all the snares of the enemy.
May your holy angels dwell here to keep us in peace
and may your blessing be upon us evermore. Amen.

Anon

ON LEAVING A MUCH LOVED HOME

Pilgrim God, your Son had no place to lay his head,
and lived the life of an itinerant preacher.
But we have put down roots in this place;
the now empty rooms echo with memories.
It's so hard to move on, to let go.
Please bless us as we turn the key
to lock the door for the very last time.
Help us to know that you journey with us,
and bless those who will make our old house
their new home. Amen.

CROWNING THE YEAR

The church's year reflects the changing seasons and marks out the passage of time. Using seasonal prayers helps us to be more conscious of our place in the greater story of God's creation, and Jesus' birth, death and resurrection. Marking the church's year helps us to live more mindfully and puts our petty irritations and concerns into proportion in the context of eternity.

I am the Alpha and the Omega,
the first and the last,
the beginning and the end.
Revelation 22:13 NRSV

DURING ADVENT

Lord Jesus, light of the world,
blessed is Gabriel, who brought good news,
blessed is Mary, your mother and ours.
Bless your Church, preparing for Christmas;
and bless us your children, who long for your coming.
Amen.
Times and Seasons

AT CHRISTMAS

May Christ the Son of God, born of Mary,
fill us with his grace
to trust his promises and obey his will;
And may the blessing of God almighty,
the Father, the Son, and the Holy Spirit,
be among us and remain with us always.
Times and Seasons

FOR A CHRISTMAS TREE

Lord our God
we praise you for the light of creation:
the sun, the moon, and the stars of the night.

We praise you for the light of Israel:
the Law, the prophets, and the wisdom of the
Scriptures.

We praise you for Jesus Christ, your Son:
Emmanuel, God-with-us, the Prince of Peace,
who fills us with the wonder of your love.

Lord God,
may your blessing come upon us
as we illumine this tree.
May the light and cheer it gives
be a sign of the joy that fills our hearts.
May all who delight in this tree
come to the knowledge and joy of salvation.

We ask this through Christ our Lord. Amen.
The Order of St Benedict

AT EPIPHANY

May Christ our Lord,
to whom kings bowed down in worship and offered gifts,
reveal to us his glory
and pour upon us the riches of his grace;
And may the blessing of God almighty,
the Father, the Son, and the Holy Spirit,
be among us and remain with us always.

Times and Seasons

DURING LENT

May Christ give us grace to grow in holiness,
to deny ourselves, take up our cross, and follow him;
And may the blessing of God almighty,
the Father, the Son, and the Holy Spirit,
be among us and remain with us always.

Times and Seasons

AT EASTER

May the God who shakes heaven and earth,
whom death could not contain,
who lives to disturb and heal us,
bless us with power to go forth
and proclaim the Gospel. Amen.

Iona Community

FROM ASCENSION TO PENTECOST

May the ascended Christ,
who promised to be with us to the end of the age
make us bold in our witness
and faithful to our calling;
And may the blessing of God almighty,
the Father, the Son, and the Holy Spirit,
be among us and remain with us always.

AT PENTECOST

May the Spirit,
who hovered over the waters
when the world was created,
breathe into us the life he gives.

May the Spirit,
who overshadowed the Virgin
when the eternal Son came among us,
make us joyful in the service of the Lord.

May the Spirit,
who set the Church on fire
upon the Day of Pentecost,
bring the world alive with the love of the risen Christ.

And may the blessing of God almighty,
the Father, the Son, and the Holy Spirit,
be among us and remain with us always.

Common Worship

AT HARVEST

May God our creator,
who clothes the lilies and feeds the birds of the air,
bestow on us his care
and increase the harvest of our righteousness;
And may the blessing of God almighty,
the Father, the Son, and the Holy Spirit,
be among us and remain with us always.

Times and Seasons

ALL SAINTS

For all the saints who from their labours rest,
who thee by faith before the world confessed,
thy name, O Jesus, be for ever blest. Alleluia.

O blest communion, fellowship divine!
we feebly struggle, they in glory shine;
yet all are one in thee, for all are thine. Alleuia.

The golden evening brightens in the west;
soon, soon to faithful warriors comes their rest;
sweet is the calm of Paradise the blest. Alleluia.

From earth's wide bounds,
from ocean's farthest coast,
through gates of pearl streams in the countless host,
singing to Father, Son and Holy Ghost. Alleluia.

W. Walsham How (1823–1897) (Common Praise)

FROM ALL SAINTS TO ADVENT

May God give us
his comfort and his peace,
his light and his joy,
in this world and the next;
And may the blessing of God almighty,
the Father, the Son, and the Holy Spirit,
be among us and remain with us always.

Times and Seasons

LET US BLESS THE LORD

*The seventeenth century Westminster Catechism begins,
'What is the chief end of man?' and the reply is quite
simply, 'To glorify God and to enjoy him forever.' Those
words are as true today as they were when they were first
written. We are most fully human when we are alive to the
presence of God, and when we, in response to God's many
blessings towards us, learn to bless him in return.*

A GENERAL THANKSGIVING
(from The Book of Common Prayer)

Almighty God, Father of all mercies,
We thine unworthy servants do give thee
most humble and hearty thanks
for all thy goodness and loving kindness
to us and to all men.
We bless thee for our creation, preservation
and all the blessings of this life;
but above all, for thine inestimable love
in the redemption of the world
by our Lord Jesus Christ:
for the means of grace, and for the hope of glory.
And, we beseech thee,
give us that due sense of all thy mercies,
that our hearts may be unfeignedly thankful,
and that we shew forth thy praise,
not only with our lips
but in our lives;
by giving up ourselves to thy service;
and by walking before thee
in holiness and righteousness all our days;
through Jesus Christ our Lord,

to whom with thee and the Holy Ghost
be all honour and glory,
world without end. Amen.

Now thank we all our God
with heart and hands and voices,
who wondrous things hath done,
in whom his world rejoices;
who from our mother's arms
hath blessed us on our way
with countless gifts of love,
and still is ours today.

All praise and thanks to God
the Father now be given,
the Son, and him who reigns
with them in highest heaven,
the one eternal God,
whom heaven and earth adore;
for thus it was, is now,
and shall be evermore. Amen.

Martin Rinkart (1586–1649)
tr Catherine Winkworth (1827–1878)
(Common Praise)

I will bless the Lord at all times;
his praise shall continually be in my mouth.

Psalm 34:1 NRSV

A PRAYER OF THANKSGIVING

God of wisdom and love,
giver of all good things,
we thank you for your loving-kindness,
and for your constant care over all creation.

We bless you for the gift of life,
for your guiding hand upon us,
and your sustaining love within us.

We thank you for friendship and duty,
for good hopes and precious memories,
for the joys that cheer us,
and the trials that teach us to trust in you.

We bless you for Jesus Christ,
your Son, our Saviour,
for the living presence of your Spirit,

for your Church, the body of Christ,
for the ministry of Word and Sacrament
and all the means of grace.

In our weakness, you are our strength;
in our darkness, light;
in our sorrows, comfort and peace.
From everlasting to everlasting
you are our God,
Father, Son and Holy Spirit,
one God, glorified for ever. Amen.

Church of Scotland

Rejoice in the Lord always; again I will say rejoice.
Let your gentleness be known to everyone.
The Lord is near.
Do not worry about anything, but in everything
by prayer and supplication with thanksgiving,
let your requests be made known to God.
And the peace of God,
which surpasses all understanding,
will guard your heart and your mind in Christ Jesus.

Philippians 4:4–7 NRSV

All the blessings we enjoy are Divine deposits, committed to our trust on this condition, that they should be dispensed for the benefit of our neighbours.

John Calvin (1509–1564)

Blessing is at the end of the road. And that which is at the end of the road influences everything that takes place along the road. The end shapes the means.
As Catherine of Siena said, 'All the way to heaven is heaven.' A joyful end requires a joyful means.
Bless the Lord.

Eugene Peterson

INDEX OF FIRST LINES

INDEX OF AUTHORS AND SOURCES

ACKNOWLEDGEMENTS

The compiler and publisher gratefully acknowledge permission to reproduce copyright material in this anthology. Every effort has been made to trace copyright holders. If there are any inadvertent omissions we apologize to those concerned; please send information to the publisher who will make a full acknowledgement in future editions.

Scripture quotations from the Revised Standard Version and the New Revised Standard Version are copyright © 1989, 1995 by division of Christian Education of the National Council of Churches in the United States of America and used by permission. All rights reserved.

Scripture taken from *The Message* is copyright © 1993, 1994, 1995, 1996, 2000, 2001, 2002. Used by permission of NavPress Publishing Group.

The Archbishops' Council of the Church of England: *Common Worship: Services and Prayers* (2000) (pp. 5, 15, 65) *Common Worship: Times and Seasons* (2006) (pp. 61, 63, 66, 68)

Bishop Michael Turnbull: (pp. 28, 41)

Cairns Publications: from Jim Cotter, *Prayer at Night* (2003) (p. 15) from Jim Cotter, *Prayer at Day's Dawning* (2001) (p. 12)

InterVarsity Press: from Eugene Peterson, *A Long Obedience in the Same Direction* (2000) (pp. 2, 74)

National Conference of Catholic Bishops: from The Order of St Benedict, *Book of Blessings* (1989) (p. 62)

The Rt Revd Graham James: (p. 14)

Saint Andrew Press: *Book of Common Order of the Church of Scotland* (1994) (pp. 5, 73)

SPCK: from St Hilda Community, *Women Included* (1996) (p. 5)

Wild Goose Resource Group: from The Iona Community, *A Wee Worship Book* (1989) (p. 16) from The Iona Community, Iona *Abbey Worship Book* (2001) (p. 39)